The Tiny Ember

The Tiny Ember

Matthew Petchinsky

1

The Tiny Ember: Pocket Motivation for Cold Days
By: Matthew Petchinsky

Disclaimer

The Tiny Ember: Pocket Motivation for Cold Days is a creative self-help and motivational guide designed to inspire personal reflection, emotional resilience, and inner momentum during colder seasons and holiday slowdowns. The techniques, metaphors, exercises, and practices described in this book are intended for **general informational, inspirational, and creative purposes only**.

This book does **not** provide medical, psychological, psychiatric, therapeutic, financial, or professional advice. Nothing in these pages is meant to diagnose, treat, cure, or prevent any disease, mental health condition, or physical ailment. Any references to "inner fire," "energetic warmth," "motivation rituals," "seasonal reset practices," or similar terms are **symbolic frameworks** meant to help readers think more deeply about their lives and choices. They are not claims of supernatural, spiritual, psychological, or physiological outcomes.

Readers should consult licensed professionals—including medical doctors, mental health providers, therapists, or financial experts—before making any decisions that could affect their physical health, mental well-being, financial situation, or long-term safety. If you are experiencing acute distress, depression, medical concerns, or crisis-level symptoms, please contact a qualified professional immediately.

All exercises in this book are voluntary and should be adapted to your personal situation, comfort level, and physical limitations. If any practice causes discomfort, emotional difficulty, or physical strain, stop immediately. The author is not responsible for how readers choose to interpret, apply, or use the material presented.

Any resemblance to real individuals, events, or situations is coincidental. This book is **not** connected to or endorsed by any scientific, religious, therapeutic, corporate, or institutional body. It is offered solely as a source of encouragement, creativity, and seasonal guidance.

By reading this book, you acknowledge that you are doing so of your own free will and understand that the contents are inspirational in nature. You agree that neither the author nor the publisher shall be held liable for any damages, losses, or adverse outcomes resulting from the use, misuse, or interpretation of the material.

May this tiny ember remind you that your inner warmth is your own—light it responsibly, and let it guide you through the cold days with clarity, intention, and self-honor.

Introduction – Finding Heat in the Hard Season

Winter changes people.

It slows the world down, tightens the air, and asks us to move through our days with heavier breath. For some, winter is a welcome pause—a chance to rest, gather, and reflect. But for many, it becomes a season where motivation thins out like daylight, where purpose feels harder to touch, and where our inner fire dwindles to a flicker. The holiday rush can drain our energy, and the cold can make goals feel distant, overwhelming, or forgotten. Even the most driven people can find themselves moving slower, thinking heavier, or doubting their momentum.

But every flame—no matter how small—has a choice: to burn out or to be protected.

This tiny book is that protection.

This is your ember.

The Tiny Ember was created to help you locate warmth within yourself when the world gets cold. Not the kind of fiery motivation that burns too bright and too fast—this book is not about hype, adrenaline, or pushing yourself to exhaustion. Instead, these pages explore a different kind of fire: the quiet, sustainable, renewable warmth that comes from intention, meaning, and small but steady progress.

Winter invites introspection, but it also tests resilience. The slowdown in work, the increase in obligations, the holiday emotional weight, the shift in routine—it all creates friction that dims the inner spark. You may feel less driven. You may feel tired earlier. You may lose track of your long-term vision. You may even question your purpose entirely. None of this means your fire is gone. It means the season is asking you to tend it differently.

Throughout this book, you will learn how to cultivate **pocket-sized motivation**—tiny rituals, quick mindset shifts, and simple but powerful reminders you can carry with you anytime. These practices are designed for the real world: for those working through exhaustion, financial pressure, emotional overload, short days, and long nights. They meet you exactly where you are, without requiring you to become someone different.

You will discover how to:

- *Create warmth in small moments,* even when the day feels cold.
- *Reignite purpose* without overwhelming yourself.
- *Build micro-habits* that feel natural in slower seasons.
- *Reconnect to meaning* when routines crumble or motivation scatters.
- *Keep momentum alive* during holidays, interruptions, and setbacks.
- *Trust your inner flame,* even when it's dim.

Each chapter is intentionally short, gentle, and implementable. Think of them as sparks: not enough to blaze into a bonfire, but enough to remind you that the fire is still there—and you are capable of feeding it.

This book is meant to fit in your pocket, your bag, or your winter coat. It's the companion you pull out when you're tired, discouraged, or unsure what to do next. When you read it, imagine cupping your hands around a small ember, shielding it from the wind, giving it space to glow again.

If the cold season has made you slow down, question yourself, or temporarily forget your strength, you are not alone. Winter affects every human differently, but every human carries a fire inside them. You do too.

Let this be the moment you reclaim it.
Let this be the season where your small ember becomes steady again.
Let this book be the warmth you return to whenever the world grows cold.

Your fire is not gone.
It is waiting.

Welcome to **The Tiny Ember**. Let's find your heat again.

Chapter 1 – The Spark That Refuses to Die

There is a moment, usually in the quiet of a cold morning or in the stillness of a winter night, when you feel something inside you withdraw. The world moves slower in the hard season, and often your energy moves with it. But beneath the exhaustion, beneath the numbness, beneath the strain of simply getting through the day, there is a small spark that refuses to go out. It is not loud or demanding. It does not roar or blaze. But it is persistent—almost stubborn—about staying alive. This spark is the foundation of your resilience, the part of you that will not surrender even when everything feels still and frozen.

Winter reveals who you are without the external noise. When the sunlight fades early and the routines of the year wind down, what's left is your internal core—your identity stripped of distractions. This quieter version of you is not weaker; it is simply more exposed. And in that exposure, the spark shows itself. Even if you've felt disconnected from your goals, or too drained to care, or too overwhelmed to try, the truth is simple: your spark is still there, waiting for you to notice it again.

The cold season often tricks us into believing our motivation has disappeared. But more often than not, it hasn't vanished—it has simply retreated, storing itself like an ember beneath ash. This is a natural response to seasonal pressure, emotional overload, or the holiday shift in routines. Instead of forcing yourself into action, Chapter 1 invites you to observe your inner fire with gentleness. The spark that remains—however small—is proof of your continuity. It is the part of you that says, *I still want better. I still believe in myself. I still care.*

When you begin to look for that spark intentionally, you start to build a relationship with your inner fire again. You learn its language: subtle nudges, small urges to move forward, quiet reminders of what matters. And as you learn to recognize these signals, you discover that the spark doesn't need to be large to be powerful. Even the smallest ember can grow when given air, attention, and protection. Your task in this chapter is not to generate a blazing fire but to honor the tiny ember that already exists.

Every winter, every slowdown, every emotional dip creates an illusion that you've lost your drive permanently. But this is temporary. Your internal spark is stronger than the season, stronger than the cold, stronger than fatigue. It has survived every difficult winter you've lived through, every setback you've endured, every moment where you thought you were done. You are here because the spark stayed with you. And now, with a little intention, you can help it glow again.

This chapter sets the tone for the rest of the book: a reminder that your motivation is not gone—it is simply quieter right now. You are not starting from zero. You are starting from an ember. And embers are incredibly powerful when protected. You don't have to be fully on fire to be moving forward. You only need to notice the spark that refuses to die.

Warmth in Small Moments

Warmth returns in tiny doses: a favorite blanket, a cup of hot tea, a single clear breath, a memory that makes you smile, a step taken even when you didn't want to move. When you deliberately notice these small moments, you begin teaching your mind that warmth still exists, even in winter.

Reignite Purpose

Your purpose doesn't need to be epic right now; it only needs to be remembered. Spend time recalling *why* you care about your goals. A spark grows the moment you reconnect to the original reason you started.

Micro-Habit: The One-Minute Flame

Choose one small, repeatable action that takes less than a minute—stretching, writing one sentence, drinking water intentionally, or setting a micro-goal. This keeps the ember alive without overwhelming you.

Reconnect to Meaning

Meaning is rediscovered in stillness. Reflect on what brings you comfort, joy, or a sense of personal identity. When meaning becomes clear, motivation follows naturally.

Keep Momentum Alive

Momentum in the winter season is not about speed—it's about continuity. Even the smallest action keeps the ember from fading. One step counts. One effort counts. One spark counts.

Trust Your Inner Flame

You have survived every cold season before. That alone is proof that your spark is trustworthy. Believe that your inner flame knows how to return to life, even when you can't see it clearly.

Exercises

Exercise 1: Identify Your Ember

Write down three things—memories, goals, sensations, or hopes—that prove your spark is still alive. These can be tiny, quiet, or soft. The point is to acknowledge them.

Exercise 2: Winter Warmth Scan

Throughout one full day, take note of every moment that brings warmth—physical, emotional, or mental. Record at least five. These moments are fuel for your spark.

Exercise 3: The One-Sentence Purpose

Complete this sentence:

"I still care because..."

Let it be honest. Let it be imperfect. This becomes your winter purpose anchor.

Meditation – The Ember in Your Hands

Close your eyes and imagine holding a small glowing ember in your palms. Feel its warmth—not burning, just steady. Picture your breath gently feeding it, each inhale pulling it closer to life, each exhale calming its glow. See yourself shielding it from cold winds with your hands. This ember is you. This ember is your momentum. Stay with it for 1–2 minutes, simply breathing and protecting it.

Journal Prompts

1. When have I felt my internal spark the strongest this year?
2. What parts of myself feel dim or quiet right now?
3. What tiny action always brings me comfort, no matter what?
4. Why do I think my spark has retreated this season?
5. What is one thing I still deeply care about?
6. How do I know that my motivation isn't gone, just resting?
7. What winter routines or memories warm me emotionally?
8. What small change would make this season feel a little easier?
9. What am I avoiding, and why?
10. What does "protecting my spark" look like in daily life?

Closing Reflection

Your spark has never abandoned you—it has simply changed shape for the season. Winter slows the body, quiets the mind, and dims the day, but it cannot extinguish the inner flame that has carried you through every hardship. Take this chapter as your reminder that even the faintest ember contains enough power to ignite new strength. Treat your spark with respect, patience, and gentleness. As you move forward, trust that this tiny ember will grow—not because you force it to, but because you choose to notice it. The hard season cannot defeat a spark that refuses to die.

Chapter 2 – Fuel Sources: What Actually Recharges You

Most people think motivation fails because they aren't trying hard enough, but the truth is simpler: you cannot run on an empty internal battery. Winter requires more energy than it appears—emotionally, mentally, and physically. The shorter days disrupt your rhythm, the colder temperatures slow your body, and the holiday season drains your attention in dozens of small, invisible ways. If your fire feels weak, it's not a flaw in your character. It's a signal that your system is asking for refueling. And just like a fire needs more than one ingredient to burn, so do you.

In this season, recharging becomes a necessity, not a luxury. Yet many people don't know what *actually* replenishes them. They default to distractions—scrolling, snacking, or numbing—to escape the discomfort of low energy. But escape is not fuel. Real fuel is made of activities, environments, and mindsets that *return* energy to you instead of draining it. This chapter helps you identify your personal fuel sources—the things that nourish your inner spark instead of depleting it.

It's important to understand that energy replenishment is not universal. What restores one person may exhaust another. This is why self-awareness becomes a winter survival skill. When you understand what elevates your emotional temperature, you no longer waste time chasing the wrong kinds of fuel. You begin to design your days around actions that support your inner fire. You tune into what warms your spirit instead of what merely distracts it.

Some fuel sources subtle—small sensory comforts, quiet moments of clarity, simple acts of gentleness toward yourself. Others are more dynamic—movement, creativity, connection, or meaningful solitude. Winter often convinces us that we have no energy to start, but the trick is not in starting big. It's in starting with the right fuel. When you give your energy the right ingredients, the spark strengthens without force.

Once you identify your real fuel sources, your inner life becomes easier to navigate. You learn what to give yourself when you're tired, where to find warmth when you feel numb, and how to restore your drive when the world feels heavy. You develop a winter toolkit unique to your emotional wiring. And instead of fighting the season, you begin to flow with it.

This chapter teaches you to stop relying on willpower alone. Willpower burns out quickly in the cold season. But the right fuel sources keep your ember alive with ease, steadiness, and longevity. Your spark can only grow when you nourish it intentionally. And the better you understand what feeds your inner fire, the easier winter becomes.

Warmth in Small Moments

Look for tiny signals of warmth: a sound you enjoy, a scent that calms you, a five-minute break that softens tension, or a piece of music that lifts your chest. Each small source is a quiet recharge.

Reignite Purpose

Purpose is reignited when you deliberately reconnect with what energizes you—not what you think *should* energize you. Let your real, lived experiences guide you to what genuinely fills your tank.

Micro-Habit: The 90-Second Reset

Take 90 seconds each day to do something that gives you even a spark of energy—stretch, breathe, sip warm tea, write a single line, or step outside for cold air clarity. These micro-refuels keep your ember from fading.

Reconnect to Meaning

Reflect on what activities make you feel more like yourself. Meaning and motivation return naturally when you engage with the things that restore your identity.

Keep Momentum Alive

Momentum is preserved by consistent refueling. Even one moment of recharging each day protects you from energy crashes. Small inputs prevent total burnout.

Trust Your Inner Flame

Your body and intuition know what feeds you. If something feels nourishing, trust it. If something drains you, allow yourself to step away. Your flame is wiser than you think.

Twelve Things That Actually Fuel You

1. Gentle Movement

Slow stretching, a short walk, or loosening your shoulders sends fresh oxygen through your body and clears mental fog. Movement wakes the ember without overwhelming you—perfect for winter sluggishness.

2. Warm, Comforting Sensations

A heated drink, a warm blanket, a hot shower, or sunlight through a window calms your nervous system. Physical warmth tells your brain, *You're safe,* which restores emotional energy.

3. Quiet, Uninterrupted Solitude

A few minutes alone without noise refills attention. Solitude restores clarity, helps you think your own thoughts again, and reduces the drain from constant stimulation.

4. Creative Expression

Writing, drawing, crafting, or brainstorming ignites inner aliveness. Creativity isn't about talent—it's about releasing the pressure that builds when your emotions have nowhere to go.

5. Meaningful Connection

A sincere conversation, a supportive message, or time with someone who makes you feel understood recharges emotional energy. Being witnessed restores motivation.

6. Nature Contact

Even in winter, a cold breeze, a bare tree, or stepping outside for one minute resets your rhythms. Nature grounds you, stabilizes mood, and reminds you that cycles of rest and renewal are natural.

7. Purpose Reminders

Reading your goals, looking at a vision board, or recalling why you care reignites emotional fire. Purpose is fuel—without it, motivation collapses.

8. Clean, Organized Space

Tidying a table, clearing a corner, or making your bed creates mental space. Clutter subtly drains you; order gives your mind room to breathe.

9. Nourishing Food & Hydration

Eating warm, grounding meals and drinking intentional water restores physical stamina. Winter dehydration is common, and it directly lowers motivation.

10. Mini Achievements

Completing one tiny task—sending an email, washing one dish, or writing one line—gives your brain a dopamine lift. Small wins generate bigger ones.

11. Rest Without Guilt

Intentional rest (not avoidance) rebuilds mental reserves. When you allow yourself to pause without shame, your spark strengthens instead of shrinking.

12. Inner Stillness

Breathwork, reflection, silence, prayer, meditation, or simply sitting with your thoughts reconnects you to your internal compass. Stillness is the purest fuel for the returning flame.

The Shadow Side of Energy: Why You Must Know What Drains You

Fuel alone isn't enough.

To keep your inner ember alive, you must also understand the forces that quietly weaken it. Drains are the opposite of fuel—they steal warmth, scatter focus, and dim your inner fire without warning. Most people underestimate their drains because they seem small, routine, or harmless... yet these are often the exact habits, environments, and emotional patterns that extinguish motivation faster than winter wind.

When you learn to recognize what drains you, you gain power. You stop blaming yourself for feeling unmotivated and start seeing the *real causes*. You begin protecting your spark instead of exposing it to everything and everyone. You build a winter life that supports you, not one that sabotages you.

This list isn't here to shame you; it's here to free you.

The moment you understand your drains, you can prevent energy loss before it happens—and your tiny ember finally has the chance to grow.

Twelve Things That Drain You (with Descriptions)

1. Emotional Overload

Taking on too many feelings—your own or other people's—burns through energy fast. Winter amplifies emotional sensitivity, making this drain even more intense.

2. Cluttered Spaces

Physical mess creates mental chaos. Even if you ignore it, your brain doesn't; it constantly processes the disorder, draining your clarity and peace.

3. Negative Self-Talk

Harsh inner criticism freezes motivation in place. When your mind attacks your progress, the spark dims quickly.

4. Overcommitment

Saying "yes" to everyone leaves no energy for yourself. Too many obligations scatter your focus and wear out your inner flame.

5. Unrested Body

Lack of sleep, irregular rest, or pushing through fatigue drains your physical fire. Winter already pulls your energy downward; ignoring rest multiplies the drain.

6. Digital Overstimulation

Constant notifications, endless scrolling, and overstimulating content exhaust your brain. The illusion of "rest" online is actually silent burnout.

7. Ignoring Basic Needs

Skipping meals, delaying water, avoiding movement—these small neglects cause big energy crashes. Your spark depends on your physical foundation.

8. Cold Environments Without Comfort

Being physically cold tightens muscles, slows circulation, and lowers mood. Without warmth, your mind works harder and drains faster.

9. Tension & Unreleased Stress

Pent-up stress burns energy in the background like a leak in your emotional fuel tank. It accumulates until your body feels heavy and your motivation disappears.

10. Unresolved Problems

Loose ends, unfinished tasks, and lingering conflicts quietly drain your attention. They hover in your mental space, making it hard to focus or feel motivated.

11. Comparing Yourself to Others

Comparison steals self-worth and turns your spark against itself. The more you measure yourself by someone else's fire, the dimmer your own becomes.

12. Doing Things That Aren't Yours to Carry

Taking responsibility for things beyond your role—fixing other people's problems, carrying their expectations, or living by someone else's script—drains your identity. And when your identity weakens, so does your flame.

Exercises

Exercise 1: Energy Audit

List ten things that drain you and ten things that energize you. Notice patterns and write one sentence describing your personal winter fuel profile.

Exercise 2: Five-Minute Refill

Choose one energizing activity from your audit and practice it for five minutes today. Observe what changes, even slightly.

Exercise 3: Fuel Sorting

Create two columns: *Real Fuel* and *False Fuel.*
Write down activities that truly replenish you vs. ones that only distract you. This becomes your winter toolkit.

Meditation – The Fuel Breath

Sit comfortably and imagine breathing in warmth with every inhale. See it as a soft golden light entering your chest. On each exhale, imagine releasing cold, dull, heavy air—the tiredness, stress, and emotional chill. Continue for one to two minutes, letting the warmth expand gently inside you.

Journal Prompts

1. What activities restore me faster than anything else?
2. What drains me more quickly than I admit?
3. When do I feel most alive during winter?
4. What comforts feel nourishing instead of numbing?
5. Which people warm my spirit, and which cool it?
6. What small sensory experiences help me feel grounded?
7. What false fuel do I rely on when I'm tired?
8. What energizing habit can I add to my daily routine?
9. When was the last time I felt fully recharged?
10. What does my inner fire need the most this week?

Closing Reflection

You cannot navigate winter on empty reserves. Your spark strengthens only when you give it the right materials. By learning what actually recharges you, you take control of your inner fire and free yourself from the exhaustion cycle. Fuel is not about indulgence—it is about survival, clarity, and self-respect. Treat your energy as something sacred. As you move forward into the colder chapters of the season, remember: the spark is already inside you. Your job now is to give it what it needs to glow.

Chapter 3 – Ember Discipline: Small Actions, Big Warmth

Winter has a way of convincing you that only dramatic effort counts—that if you can't produce something huge, it's not worth trying at all. But the truth is that discipline in the cold season is *not* built from big leaps. It's created from tiny, consistent actions that feed your inner ember just enough to keep it glowing. Think of ember discipline as the ability to build meaningful warmth from the smallest sparks. It's a discipline of gentleness, of low-pressure momentum, of choosing "just a little" instead of giving up entirely.

Small actions matter more in winter because your energy economy changes. When sunlight fades early and emotional demands rise, your nervous system becomes more sensitive to pressure. Winter is not the season for towering expectations; it's the season for steady maintenance. Ember discipline honors your changing capacity by asking less of you while giving you more in return. Every small action becomes a protective shield over your spark, preventing it from dimming beneath the weight of fatigue or seasonal overwhelm.

This is the chapter where you train yourself to see the power of "small but consistent." A single warm breath, one organized corner of your home, a tiny piece of a goal, five minutes of movement, one gentle affirmation—these are not insignificant. They are miniature acts of resistance against emotional cold. When practiced repeatedly, they create momentum that feels organic instead of forced. Ember discipline teaches your spark that it is safe to grow again, even when the world is heavy.

The challenge of this chapter is reprogramming the belief that progress must be dramatic to be real. Big achievements are the result of tiny steps repeated dozens or hundreds of times. Winter is the perfect season to embrace that truth. When you shift from urgency to consistency, you stop burning out and start building a sustainable fire. You move from perfectionism to presence. From discouragement to direction. From exhaustion to steady renewal.

What you practice in ember discipline becomes the foundation for your strongest seasons. By honoring small actions now, you create a mindset that carries you through challenges, setbacks, and emotional dips in future months. You learn to trust yourself again—not because you're doing everything perfectly, but because you're doing something consistently. Each small action is a message to your spark: *You matter. I'm tending you. I'm not leaving you behind.*

This chapter is a quiet but powerful turning point. It is the shift from waiting for motivation to creating it. Ember discipline is not about force—it is about relationship. You show up for your spark, a little at a time, and watch it warm your entire life.

Warmth in Small Moments

Winter rewards small tenderness. Brew a warm drink, step into a heated shower, light a candle, or sit with a soft blanket. Each tiny moment of warmth reinforces your ember and reminds your body that comfort still exists.

Reignite Purpose

Reignite purpose by shrinking it. Instead of asking, "What is my big mission?" ask, "What small piece of my purpose can I touch today?" Purpose grows faster when approached in fragments.

Micro-Habit: The Two-Minute Start

Commit to doing just two minutes of anything that nourishes your spark—writing, cleaning, stretching, reading, or goal work. Most people find that two minutes naturally becomes five or ten, but even if it stays small, it still builds discipline.

Reconnect to Meaning

Meaning is rediscovered when you take one purposeful action each day. A tiny action toward something you care about creates a thread of meaning that warms the coldest days.

Keep Momentum Alive

Momentum thrives on tiny repetitions. Even if you progress by only 1%, you build trust in your ability to continue. Winter momentum isn't about speed—it's about continuity.

Trust Your Inner Flame

Trust that your spark understands slow seasons. It doesn't demand intensity—it asks for presence. Every small action you take is proof that your inner flame is capable of surviving any winter.

Exercises

Exercise 1: The Smallest Step Strategy

Choose a current goal and break it into the tiniest possible action—something that takes 1–3 minutes. Do that action today. Notice how your spark responds.

Exercise 2: Winter Micro-Routine

Create a daily winter routine containing three micro-actions under two minutes each. This becomes your ember discipline ritual.

Exercise 3: The "Bare Minimum" Habit

Identify one area of your life (health, creativity, organization, finances, etc.). Create a bare-minimum habit that keeps it alive through the cold season.

Meditation – The Candle That Doesn't Quit

Visualize a single candle in a dark winter room. The flame is small but steady. Watch how even this tiny light softens the space, warms the air, and holds its shape despite the cold around it. Imagine that candle as your discipline—quiet, persistent, alive. Breathe with it for one minute, feeling the steadiness transfer into you.

Journal Prompts

1. What small daily actions make me feel the most capable?
2. Where do I pressure myself to "go big" instead of starting small?
3. What is one area of my life that would benefit from micro-actions?
4. How do I define discipline during winter?
5. What tiny habit would bring the most warmth to my day?
6. What small action could help me reconnect with my goals?
7. Why do I sometimes underestimate small progress?
8. Which small routine could anchor my mornings?
9. Which small routine could calm my evenings?
10. What does my spark feel like when I honor it consistently?

Closing Reflection

Your spark grows through what you practice, not what you dream. Small actions may seem insignificant, but they are the heartbeat of winter resilience. Ember discipline transforms you from someone who waits for energy into someone who generates it—slowly, gently, intentionally. Every tiny step is an act of loyalty to your inner fire. As you move through this season, remember: small warmth is still warmth. And often, it is enough to carry you through the coldest days.

Chapter 4 – Protecting Your Inner Flame From Others

Not all winters come from the weather. Some are born from the people around you—those who drain your energy, diminish your enthusiasm, or unintentionally smother your spark under the weight of their expectations, moods, or demands. While your inner flame is powerful, it is also sensitive. It responds to emotional climates, social dynamics, and the ways you are treated. Protecting it is not selfish; it is essential. A flame left unshielded cannot survive the wind.

Human beings naturally absorb the emotional temperatures of others. A single negative conversation can lower your motivation for the entire day. Someone else's stress can become your anxiety. Someone's criticism can dim your confidence. Someone's expectations can pressure your inner fire to burn in ways that exhaust you. Winter amplifies this effect. When your energy is already fragile, outside influence becomes even more impactful. This chapter teaches you how to notice those influences, set boundaries, and protect your warmth.

Protecting your inner flame doesn't mean you isolate yourself. It means you develop healthy filters—ways to allow warmth, support, and connection in while keeping out anything that chills your spirit. This requires awareness: noticing who expands your energy and who compresses it. It requires courage: saying no when you once said yes, stepping back when you once stepped in, and choosing your peace even when others don't understand.

There will always be people who move through life like drafts—pulling warmth away from you without trying. There will also be people who bring fire, energy, and encouragement. Your task is to distinguish the two. This chapter invites you to build a personal protection strategy, a winter shield for your spark. Because no matter how small your ember is, it deserves to be guarded with intention.

Learning to protect yourself from the emotional temperature of others doesn't make you unkind; it makes you wise. You cannot sustain motivation in winter if you allow everyone else's storms to blow through your internal world. You cannot nurture your ember if you allow it to be exposed to every gust of negativity. And you cannot grow your flame if you are constantly relighting it after others extinguish it.

Your inner fire belongs to you. No one else gets to decide how you burn, how bright you become, or how much energy you give away. This chapter is your shield—your guide to protecting your flame without guilt, without apology, and without losing the warmth that makes you who you are.

12 Ways to Protect Your Inner Flame (with Descriptions)

1. Limit Exposure to Negative People

You don't have to cut everyone out—just reduce the time spent with those who consistently drain your emotional warmth.

2. Say "No" Without Explaining

Your flame dims every time you justify your boundaries. A simple "No, I can't" is enough.

3. Keep Your Goals Private Around Critical People

Not everyone deserves access to your spark. Protect your dreams by sharing them only with those who support you.

4. Step Away When Conversations Turn Heavy

You don't have to absorb emotional burdens. Excuse yourself gently when things become overwhelming.

5. Use Emotional Filters

Before accepting someone's words, ask yourself: *Is this about me or them?* Most negativity belongs to the person speaking it.

6. Maintain Warm Spaces

Create physical environments (tidy, warm, calm) that protect your spark from being influenced by external chaos.

7. Observe Before You Absorb

Pause when people are intense, dramatic, or demanding. Notice what's happening—don't internalize it.

8. Prioritize Your Energy First

If your flame is low, meeting everyone else's needs becomes impossible. Refuel yourself before helping others.

9. Avoid Arguing With Cold People

You cannot convince someone who is committed to misunderstanding you. Protect your energy by walking away.

10. Set Time Limits with Draining Loved Ones

Love doesn't mean unlimited access. Time caps preserve your warmth without cutting connection.

11. Stop Over-Explaining Your Feelings

Your emotions are valid even if others don't understand. Don't shrink your flame trying to be approved.

12. Trust Your Gut Instinct About People

If someone consistently leaves you drained, your body is telling you the truth. Protect your flame accordingly.

Warmth in Small Moments

Build micro-boundaries—stepping outside for a breath, putting in headphones, pausing a conversation, or choosing not to respond immediately. Every small moment of separation preserves warmth.

Reignite Purpose

Remember that your purpose belongs to you, not to the expectations of others. Protecting your flame allows your true purpose to thrive without being shaped or minimized by external voices.

Micro-Habit: The Boundary Breath

Before interacting with someone draining, take one deep breath and silently say:

"My energy stays with me."

This tiny habit strengthens your protective shield.

Reconnect to Meaning

Meaning deepens when you choose people and environments that support your emotional temperature. Protecting your flame reconnects you to the life you actually want—not the one others push onto you.

Keep Momentum Alive

Momentum stays alive when you don't let others derail your focus. Protecting your flame is how you avoid emotional detours that cost days or weeks of motivation.

Trust Your Inner Flame

You have the right to protect your warmth. Your flame knows who helps it grow and who weakens it. Trust that instinct—it's ancient, accurate, and always guiding you.

Exercises

Exercise 1: Boundary Mapping

List three people who warm your energy and three who drain it. Write one boundary for each draining person.

Exercise 2: The Energy Shield Sentence

Write a one-sentence affirmation you repeat before difficult interactions. Example:
"Their emotions are theirs; my fire is mine."

Exercise 3: Emotional Temperature Check

After spending time with someone, ask:
"Do I feel warmer or colder?"
Record your insights for one week.

Meditation – The Shield of Light

Visualize a soft, golden barrier of warmth around your body. It glows like a gentle dome around your spark. Any negativity or coldness that reaches you dissolves before it touches your flame. This shield stays with you throughout the day.

Journal Prompts

1. Who warms my inner flame the most?
2. Who consistently chills or drains me?
3. What boundary have I been afraid to set?
4. What happens to my spark when I over-give?
5. Which relationships support my winter energy?
6. What emotional burdens am I carrying that aren't mine?
7. How do I feel when I protect my energy successfully?
8. What limiting belief makes me hesitate to set boundaries?
9. Where in my life do I need a stronger shield?
10. What would change if I protected my flame every day?

Closing Reflection

Your inner flame is sacred. Not everyone deserves access to it, and not everyone knows how to treat it with care. Protecting your spark is not about rejecting others—it's about choosing your well-being over their expectations, moods, or demands. When you shield your energy with intention, you preserve the warmth that carries you through winter and into every chapter of your life. Let your flame remain yours—steady, glowing, and fiercely protected.

Chapter 5 – Becoming Your Own Fireplace

A fireplace does more than produce heat—it creates atmosphere, safety, grounding, and centeredness. It becomes the emotional heart of a room. Winter teaches us that survival isn't just about maintaining warmth; it's about having a place to return to, a center where the cold cannot reach. When you become your own fireplace, you become the source of your own grounding. You become a generator of inner warmth that doesn't rely on external seasons, validation, or circumstances.

Becoming your own fireplace begins with the recognition that you are both the spark and the structure that protects it. You are not just the ember—you are the foundation around it. You are the stones that hold the flame upright, the walls that block out drafts, the steady architecture that turns a tiny spark into long-lasting heat. This is empowerment at its most intimate: not waiting for someone else to warm you, motivate you, or bring stability into your life, but creating those things from within.

This chapter is about building internal conditions instead of waiting for external ones. A fireplace works no matter what the weather outside is doing. Likewise, your internal grounding must work even through chaos, exhaustion, or emotional storms. You become your own source of steadiness by developing anchor habits, safe inner spaces, emotional routines, and protective structures that make you feel contained and supported. When you build these internal pillars, you no longer fear the cold—you just adapt to it.

The world will not always be gentle. People will not always be careful. Seasons will not always cooperate. Circumstances will not always align with your timing or energy. But the more you become your own fireplace, the less these fluctuations matter. You learn how to stabilize yourself in moments that once destabilized you. You learn how to recenter when life pushes you sideways. You learn how to comfort yourself without depending on things you can't control. This internal resilience is not rigid—it's warm, living, and deeply human.

Becoming your own fireplace also means building rituals of internal nourishment. A fireplace must be tended—fed, cleaned, maintained. Likewise, your inner warmth thrives through routines that make you feel calm and capable: mindful pauses, grounding breaths, expressive outlets, moments of solitude, sensory comforts, and affirmations that remind you who you are. When these become part of your daily rhythm, your presence becomes a place you can trust.

In this chapter, you will create a personal inner sanctuary powerful enough to carry you through winter and beyond. When you become your own fireplace, you no longer fear losing motivation—you know how to generate it. You no longer fear emotional cold—you know how to warm yourself. You no longer fear burnout—you know how to replenish your flame. You become your own shelter, your own heat source, and your own home.

The Qualities of a Personal Fireplace

Becoming your own fireplace means embodying specific qualities—inner traits that hold, protect, and nourish your spark. These qualities are the "architecture" of your internal hearth, shaping how you generate warmth even in the coldest seasons of life.

1. Stability

A fireplace doesn't wobble when the wind blows—and neither should your inner center. Stability anchors you so that external emotions, drama, or chaos cannot knock you off balance as easily.

2. Warmth

Warmth is the emotional heat you give yourself: kindness, gentleness, soft thoughts. It is the quality that turns self-presence into self-comfort.

3. Emotional Protection

A fireplace shields its flame from drafts. Emotional protection means creating boundaries that keep negativity, harshness, and mental clutter from extinguishing your spark.

4. Self-Sourced Comfort

A fireplace doesn't rely on outside weather to generate heat—it produces its own. When you can comfort, soothe, and reassure yourself, you no longer depend on unpredictable external factors.

5. Consistency

A fireplace maintains its flame through steady maintenance. Consistency in your habits, mindset, and small rituals allows your inner warmth to remain reliable.

6. Inner Grounding

Grounding is the foundation beneath the fire—the sense of "I am here, I am safe, I am steady." It keeps you from floating into anxiety or sinking into overwhelm.

7. Quiet Strength

A fireplace does not shout its presence; its power is subtle but undeniable. Quiet strength is the strength you hold inwardly—strength that doesn't need to be loud to be real.

8. Self-Renewal

Ashes are cleared, logs are added, and the fire revives again and again. Self-renewal is your ability to bounce back, refresh your energy, and reignite your spark with grace.

How to Build Emotional Firewood

Your fireplace needs long-burning fuel. Emotional firewood is anything that strengthens, soothes, or replenishes you from the inside out. These resources keep your spark alive when you're tired, stressed, or overwhelmed.

1. Self-Compassion

This is the softest and strongest fuel you own. When you speak to yourself with kindness, your inner flame becomes easier to sustain.

2. Structured Routines

Simple weekly or daily rhythms—like morning rituals or bedtime wind-downs—provide stability and predictability, helping your spark stay steady.

3. Sensory Comfort

Warm blankets, gentle scents, soft lights, soothing music—these sensory elements nourish your nervous system and create emotional ease.

4. Meaningful Solitude

Time with yourself allows your spark to breathe. Solitude helps you reset, reflect, and reconnect to your inner world without interruptions.

5. Clear Boundaries

Boundaries are like fire guards—they keep negativity, overcommitment, and other people's storms from dimming your flame.

6. Hope

Hope is a long-burning log—it carries you through difficult days and gives your fire something to reach toward.

7. Reflection

Journaling, thinking, or pausing to understand yourself deepens your inner warmth. Reflection clears emotional clutter and strengthens your clarity.

8. Slow Mornings

Moments without rushing give your nervous system time to settle. A slow start gives your ember space to rise gently.

9. Creative Expression

Art, writing, or building something sends fresh oxygen to your inner fire. Creativity helps you stay emotionally awake and alive.

10. Movement

Walking, stretching, or gentle activity moves stagnant energy out of your system. It's like stirring a fire to keep it glowing.

11. Connection With People Who Warm You

Supportive, kind, uplifting people add warmth to your fire instead of taking from it.

12. Rest and Retreat

Pulling back when overwhelmed is not weakness—it's maintenance. Rest keeps your fire from burning out.

The Internal Fireplace Blueprint

A fireplace doesn't appear magically—it is built with intention. The same is true for your internal hearth. This simple 5-step blueprint shows you how to construct a warm, protected, emotionally grounded inner space.

Step 1: Identify What Grounds You

Determine what makes you feel calm, safe, and centered. These become the "stones" of your internal fireplace.

Step 2: Create a Sensory Foundation

Add warmth, comfort, and soothing environmental elements—soft lighting, calming sounds, warm textures—that support your emotional state.

Step 3: Develop Emotional Rituals

Choose small daily actions, like a morning breath ritual, evening reflection practice, or grounding affirmation, that keep your flame alive.

Step 4: Build Protective Boundaries

Like a fire guard, boundaries protect your spark from drafts—negative people, overwhelming demands, and emotional chaos.

Step 5: Maintain With Gentle Consistency

A fireplace lives through maintenance, not force. Keep tending your internal warmth through small, steady habits that nourish your spark.

The Hearth Mindset Shift

Becoming your own fireplace isn't just a set of actions—it's a shift in identity. It rewrites the way you relate to your energy, motivation, and resilience.

You are not waiting for the world to warm you.

Winter may be cold, but warmth still exists—because you create it from within.

You create your own emotional climate.

The mood of others or the weight of circumstances no longer dictates how you feel inside.

You can choose your internal temperature.

Through breath, boundaries, rituals, and grounding, you decide how warm your inner world stays.

You can return to yourself when life gets cold.

Your inner fireplace becomes a safe place you can visit anytime you feel scattered or overwhelmed.

Your presence becomes a place of safety.

Your inner warmth radiates outward and eventually influences the world around you. You become the hearth in your own life—and sometimes even in the lives of others.

Warmth in Small Moments

Notice the tiny actions that make you feel grounded: sitting still for a minute, dimming the lights, playing soft music, warming your hands, or taking slow breaths. Each one builds your internal fireplace brick by brick.

Reignite Purpose

A fireplace represents consistency. Reignite your purpose by choosing steady, reliable motivations rather than dramatic surges. Purpose grows stronger when it feels like a ritual instead of a performance.

Micro-Habit: The Grounding Spark

Each morning, choose one grounding action—lighting a candle, stretching, journaling one sentence, or making your bed. This becomes your daily fireplace ignition.

Reconnect to Meaning

Meaning comes alive when you intentionally create inner spaces that feel like "home." Ask yourself what brings emotional comfort—silence, scent, order, warmth—and build those elements into your inner world.

Keep Momentum Alive

Momentum thrives in environments where you feel stable. When you cultivate an internal fireplace, momentum no longer depends on mood—it depends on structure.

Trust Your Inner Flame

Trust that you are capable of being your own warmth. You've survived every cold chapter so far, and your inner flame has guided you through each one. Trust its ability to rise again.

Exercises

Exercise 1: Build Your Inner Fireplace

List the five elements that make you feel grounded (lighting, warmth, sound, scent, movement, textures, etc.). Turn them into a daily or weekly ritual that supports your emotional center.

Exercise 2: Emotional Firewood Inventory

Write down five things that reliably refuel you emotionally. These are your "firewood"—use them intentionally during low-energy days.

Exercise 3: Create a Grounding Anchor

Choose one small object—a necklace, a stone, a keychain, a bookmark—that symbolizes warmth and stability. Hold it during stressful moments as a reminder of your inner fireplace.

Meditation – The Hearth Within

Imagine a fireplace glowing warmly inside your chest. See the brick, the stone, the soft light radiating outward. Imagine the fire gently flickering, producing steady warmth that fills your entire body. Feel the stability of this inner hearth—solid, comforting, unshakable. Sit with it for one to two minutes, letting its warmth become part of you.

Journal Prompts

1. What habits make me feel grounded and supported?
2. What emotional "bricks" do I need to build my inner fireplace?
3. When did I last feel truly safe within myself?
4. What does inner warmth feel like to me?
5. What routines help me return to center after stress?
6. Who or what disrupts my sense of internal stability?
7. What does emotional safety mean in my life right now?
8. What sensory experiences comfort me the most?
9. How can I create a daily ritual of internal warmth?
10. What would life feel like if I trusted myself completely?

Closing Reflection

A fireplace is more than a flame—it is a sanctuary, a place of return, a symbol of stability in a world that shifts constantly. As you become your own fireplace, you build a life where emotional cold can't reach you. You carry your warmth everywhere. You learn to trust your own comfort, your own grounding, and your own ability to sustain your spark. Winter becomes easier not because it changes, but because *you* do. Your inner fire becomes a home, and you become the guardian of your own warmth.

Appendix A – 31 Ember Actions

December is a month of shortened light, heightened emotion, and unpredictable energy. These 31 Ember Actions are designed to give you small, meaningful ways to nurture your inner flame every day. Each action requires very little time, but each one strengthens your emotional warmth, clarity, and sense of purpose.

Day 1 – The Candle of Intention

Light a candle and set a simple intention for the month—one sentence that represents the kind of warmth you want to build.
Purpose: Signals your ember that you are entering a season of deliberate care.

Day 2 – The Small Space Reset

Choose one tiny area—a drawer, a shelf, a corner—and tidy it.
Purpose: Clears an emotional draft and creates space for inner heat to grow.

Day 3 – Winter Breath Ritual

Take five slow breaths: inhale warmth, exhale heaviness.
Purpose: Stabilizes your nervous system and feeds your spark oxygen.

Day 4 – The Warm Drink Pause

Prepare a hot beverage intentionally. Sit with it for three undistracted minutes.
Purpose: Teaches your body to associate stillness with comfort.

Day 5 – Name Your Firewood

Write down five things that fuel you. Keep the list nearby.
Purpose: Helps you choose replenishment over instinctive numbing.

Day 6 – The Social Boundary Reset

Say “no” to one request that drains you today.

Purpose: Protects your inner flame from unnecessary cold.

Day 7 – Five-Minute Creative Spark

Write, draw, hum, craft, or brainstorm for just five minutes.

Purpose: Creativity stirs the ember in ways discipline alone cannot.

Day 8 – The Winter Walk

Step outside for 1–3 minutes. Let the cold sharpen your clarity.

Purpose: Contrasting temperature awakens your inner warmth.

Day 9 – Gratitude Embers

List three small things that brought you warmth this week.

Purpose: Anchors your awareness in emotional heat instead of emotional frost.

Day 10 – Rest Without Permission

Give yourself 10 guilt-free minutes of intentional rest.

Purpose: Rest refills your spark more than forced productivity.

Day 11 – The Warmth Playlist

Create a short playlist of songs that lift your emotional temperature.

Purpose: Sound influences the nervous system and strengthens your ember.

Day 12 – Ember Posture Check

Sit or stand with your chest open and shoulders relaxed.

Purpose: A warmed posture invites confidence and inner fire.

Day 13 – The Moment of Solitude

Spend 3–5 minutes alone with no screens, no noise.

Purpose: Solitude repairs the flame that social overwhelm damages.

Day 14 – The Kind Thought Practice

Say something gentle to yourself. One sentence.

Purpose: Self-compassion is one of the longest-burning fuels.

Day 15 – Slow Morning Minutes

Spend the first three minutes of the day moving slowly and intentionally.

Purpose: A soft start protects your spark from morning chill.

Day 16 – Fire-Safe Boundaries

Set one micro-boundary: delay a text response, limit a conversation, or pause a call.

Purpose: Reduces emotional drafts and keeps your warmth intact.

Day 17 – The Cozy Ritual

Add one cozy element to your space: soft lighting, warm socks, blankets, scent.

Purpose: Sensory comfort influences emotional stability.

Day 18 – The One-Sentence Purpose

Write one sentence beginning with: *"I care about..."*

Purpose: Refocuses your spark on meaning, not pressure.

Day 19 – Three Tiny Wins

Write down three things you accomplished today—no matter the size.

Purpose: Micro-wins produce emotional heat.

Day 20 – Release the Draft

Identify one emotional draft—an annoyance, obligation, or lingering worry—and write how you'll address or minimize it.
Purpose: Seals leaks that weaken your fire.

Day 21 – The Warm Body Ritual

Take a warm shower, bath, or foot soak.
Purpose: Physical warmth directly influences emotional warmth.

Day 22 – Speak Your Stability

Repeat this affirmation twice:
"I am my own fireplace. My warmth comes from within."
Purpose: Reinforces the identity shift cultivated in Chapter 5.

Day 23 – The Compassion Letter

Write a three-sentence note to your future self for the hard days.
Purpose: Creates an internal support system.

Day 24 – The Winter Reflection

Reflect on the previous 24 days of actions. Which warmed you the most?
Purpose: Awareness amplifies future heat.

Day 25 – Joy in Small Doses

Give yourself one tiny joy—a treat, an activity, a moment you'd forgotten.
Purpose: Tiny joys ignite bright sparks.

Day 26 – Declutter One Emotion

Write down an emotion that's been heavy. Name it. Release it.
Purpose: Emotional clarity lightens the inner load.

Day 27 – The Grounding Touchstone

Hold an object that represents stability—a stone, necklace, keychain—and breathe with it.

Purpose: Creates a tangible anchor for your inner hearth.

Day 28 – The Light Check-In

Check on your literal lighting. Adjust lamps or candles to create warmth.

Purpose: Lighting impacts mood more in winter than any other season.

Day 29 – The Gentle Reset

Reset one small area of your life: your bag, your phone photos, your desk.

Purpose: Freshness feeds the ember.

Day 30 – The Firekeeper Mindset

Ask yourself: *"How can I preserve my warmth today?"*

Purpose: Reinforces the proactive role you have in tending your flame.

Day 31 – The Ember of the New Year

Sit quietly with your inner flame. Ask:

"What warmth am I carrying into the next year?"

Let the answer rise naturally.

Purpose: Ends December with inner power, not outer pressure.

Closing Note for Appendix A

These 31 Ember Actions are not tasks or chores—they are tiny rituals that build emotional insulation during the hardest month of the year. Practice them gently, consistently, and without pressure. The warmth they generate will carry you far beyond December.

Message from the Author:

I hope you enjoyed this book, I love astrology and knew there was not a book such as this out on the shelf. I love metaphysical items as well. Please check out my other books:

-Life of Government Benefits

-My life of Hell

-My life with Hydrocephalus

-Red Sky

-World Domination:Woman's rule

-World Domination:Woman's Rule 2: The War

-Life and Banishment of Apophis: book 1

-The Kidney Friendly Diet

-The Ultimate Hemp Cookbook

-Creating a Dispensary(legally)

-Cleanliness throughout life: the importance of showering from childhood to adulthood.

-Strong Roots: The Risks of Overcoddling children

-Hemp Horoscopes: Cosmic Insights and Earthly Healing

- Celestial Hemp Navigating the Zodiac: Through the Green Cosmos

-Astrological Hemp: Aligning The Stars with Earth's Ancient Herb

-The Astrological Guide to Hemp: Stars, Signs, and Sacred Leaves

-Green Growth: Innovative Marketing Strategies for your Hemp Products and Dispensary

-Cosmic Cannabis

-Astrological Munchies

-Henry The Hemp

-Zodiacal Roots: The Astrological Soul Of Hemp

- **Green Constellations: Intersection of Hemp and Zodiac**

-Hemp in The Houses: An astrological Adventure Through The Cannabis Galaxy

-Galactic Ganja Guide

Heavenly Hemp

Zodiac Leaves
Doctor Who Astrology
Cannastrology
Stellar Satvias and Cosmic Indicas
Celestial Cannabis: A Zodiac Journey
AstroHerbology: The Sky and The Soil: Volume 1
AstroHerbology:Celestial Cannabis:Volume 2
Cosmic Cannabis Cultivation
The Starry Guide to Herbal Harmony: Volume 1
The Starry Guide to Herbal Harmony: Cannabis Universe: Volume 2
Yugioh Astrology: Astrological Guide to Deck, Duels and more
Nightmare Mansion: Echoes of The Abyss
Nightmare Mansion 2: Legacy of Shadows
Nightmare Mansion 3: Shadows of the Forgotten
Nightmare Mansion 4: Echoes of the Damned
The Life and Banishment of Apophis: Book 2
Nightmare Mansion: Halls of Despair
Healing with Herb: Cannabis and Hydrocephalus
Planetary Pot: Aligning with Astrological Herbs: Volume 1
Fast Track to Freedom: 30 Days to Financial Independence Using AI, Assets, and Agile Hustles
Cosmic Hemp Pathways
How to Become Financially Free in 30 Days: 10,000 Paths to Prosperity
Zodiacal Herbage: Astrological Insights: Volume 1
Nightmare Mansion: Whispers in the Walls
The Daleks Invade Atlantis
Henry the hemp and Hydrocephalus

10X The Kidney Friendly Diet
Cannabis Universe: Adult coloring book
Hemp Astrology: The Healing Power of the Stars

Zodiacal Herbage: Astrological Insights: Cannabis Universe: Volume 2

Planetary Pot: Aligning with Astrological Herbs: Cannabis Universes: Volume 2

Doctor Who: Convergence Protocol – The Replicator War

Nightmare Mansion: Curse of the Blood Moon

The Celestial Stoner: A Guide to the Zodiac

Cosmic Pleasures: Sex Toy Astrology for Every Sign

Hydrocephalus Astrology: Navigating the Stars and Healing Waters

Lapis and the Mischievous Chocolate Bar

Celestial Positions: Sexual Astrology for Every Sign

Apophis's Shadow Work Journal: **:** A Journey of Self-Discovery and Healing

Kinky Cosmos: Sexual Kink Astrology for Every Sign

Digital Cosmos: The Astrological Digimon Compendium

Stellar Seeds: The Cosmic Guide to Growing with Astrology

Apophis's Daily Gratitude Journal

Cat Astrology: Feline Mysteries of the Cosmos

The Cosmic Kama Sutra: An Astrological Guide to Sexual Positions

Unleash Your Potential: A Guided Journal Powered by AI Insights

Whispers of the Enchanted Grove

Cosmic Pleasures: An Astrological Guide to Sexual Kinks

369, 12 Manifestation Journal

Whisper of the nocturne journal(blank journal for writing or drawing)

The Boogey Book

Locked In Reflection: A Chastity Journey Through Locktober

Generating Wealth Quickly:How to Generate $100,000 in 24 Hours

Star Magic: Harness the Power of the Universe

The Flatulence Chronicles: A Fart Journal for Self-Discovery

The Doctor and The Death Moth

Seize the Day: A Personal Seizure Tracking Journal

The Ultimate Boogeyman Safari: A Journey into the Boogie World and Beyond

Whispers of Samhain: 1,000 Spells of Love, Luck, and Lunar Magic: Samhain Spell Book

Apophis's guides:Witch's Spellbook Crafting Guide for Halloween

Frost & Flame: The Enchanted Yule Grimoire of 1000 Winter Spells

The Ultimate Boogey Goo Guide & Spooky Activities for Halloween Fun

Harmony of the Scales: A Libra's Spellcraft for Balance and Beauty

The Enchanted Advent: 36 Days of Christmas Wonders

Nightmare Mansion: The Labyrinth of Screams

Harvest of Enchantment: 1,000 Spells of Gratitude, Love, and Fortune for Thanksgiving

The Boogey Chronicles: A Journal of Nightly Encounters and Shadowy Secrets

The 12 Days of Financial Freedom: A Step-by-Step Christmas Countdown to Transform Your Finances

Sigil of the Eternal Spiral Blank Journal

A Christmas Feast: Timeless Recipes for Every Meal

Holiday Stress-Free Solutions: A Survival Guide to Thriving During the Festive Season

Yu-Gi-Oh! Holiday Gifting Mastery: The Ultimate Guide for Fans and Newcomers Alike

Holiday Harmony: A Hydrocephalus Survival Guide for the Festive Season

Celestial Craft: The Witch's Almanac for 2025 – A Cosmic Guide to Manifestations, Moons, and Mystical Events

Doctor Who: The Toymaker's Winter Wonderland

Tulsa King Unveiled: A Thrilling Guide to Stallone's Mafia Masterpiece

Pendulum Craft: A Complete Guide to Crafting and Using Personalized Divination Tools

Nightmare Mansion: Santa's Eternal Eve

Starlight Noel: A Cosmic Journey through Christmas Mysteries

The Dark Architect: Unlocking the Blueprint of Existence

Surviving the Embrace: The Ultimate Guide to Encounters with The Hugging Molly

The Enchanted Codex: Secrets of the Craft for Witches, Wiccans, and Pagans

Harvest of Gratitude: A Complete Thanksgiving Guide

Yuletide Essentials: A Complete Guide to an Authentic and Magical Christmas

Celestial Smokes: A Cosmic Guide to Cigars and Astrology

Living in Balance: A Comprehensive Survival Guide to Thriving with Diabetes Insipidus

Cosmic Symbiosis: The Venom Zodiac Chronicles

The Cursed Paw of Ambition

Cosmic Symbiosis: The Astrological Venom Journal

Celestial Wonders Unfold: A Stargazer's Guide to the Cosmos (2024-2029)

The Ultimate Black Friday Prepper's Guide: Mastering Shopping Strategies and Savings

Cosmic Sales: The Astrological Guide to Black Friday Shopping

Legends of the Corn Mother and Other Harvest Myths

Whispers of the Harvest: The Corn Mother's Journal

The Evergreen Spellbook

The Doctor Meets the Boogeyman

The White Witch of Rose Hall's SpellBook

The Gingerbread Golem's Shadow: A Study in Sweet Darkness

The Gingerbread Golem Codex: An Academic Exploration of Sweet Myths

The Gingerbread Golem Grimoire: Sweet Magicks and Spells for the Festive Witch

The Curse of the Gingerbread Golem

10-minute Christmas Crafts for kids

Christmas Crisis Solutions: The Ultimate Last-Minute Survival Guide

Gingerbread Golem Recipes: Holiday Treats with a Magical Twist

The Infinite Key: Unlocking Mystical Secrets of the Ages

Enchanted Yule: A Wiccan and Pagan Guide to a Magical and Memorable Season

Dinosaurs of Power: Unlocking Ancient Magick

Astro-Dinos: The Cosmic Guide to Prehistoric Wisdom

Gallifrey's Yule Logs: A Festive Doctor Who Cookbook

The Dino Grimoire: Secrets of Prehistoric Magick

The Gift They Never Knew They Needed

The Gingerbread Golem's Culinary Alchemy: Enchanting Recipes for a Sweetly Dark Feast

A Time Lord Christmas: Holiday Adventures with the Doctor

Krampusproofing Your Home: Defensive Strategies for Yule

Silent Frights: A Collection of Christmas Creepypastas to Chill Your Bones

Santa Raptor's Jolly Carnage: A Dino-Claus Christmas Tale

Prehistoric Palettes: A Dino Wicca Coloring Journey

The Christmas Wishkeeper Chronicles

The Starlight Sleigh: A Holiday Journey

Elf Secrets: The True Magic of the North Pole

Candy Cane Conjurations

Cooking with Kids: Recipes Under 20 Minutes

Doctor Who: The TARDIS Confiscation

The Anxiety First Aid Kit: Quick Tools to Calm Your Mind

Frosty Whispers: A Winter's Tale

The Infinite Key: Unlocking the Secrets to Prosperity, Resilience, and Purpose

The Grasping Void: Why You'll Regret This Purchase

Astrology for Busy Bees: Star Signs Simplified

The Instant Focus Formula: Cut Through the Noise

The Secret Language of Colors: Unlocking the Emotional Codes

Sacred Fossil Chronicles: Blank Journal

The Christmas Cottage Miracle

Feeding Frenzy: Graboid-Inspired Recipes

Manifest in Minutes: The Quick Law of Attraction Guide

The Symbiote Chronicles: Doctor Who's Venomous Journey

Think Tiny, Grow Big: The Minimalist Mindset

The Energy Key: Unlocking Limitless Motivation

New Year, New Magic: Manifesting Your Best Year Yet

Unstoppable You: Mastering Confidence in Minutes

Infinite Energy: The Secret to Never Feeling Drained

Lightning Focus: Mastering the Art of Productivity in a Distracted World

Saturnalia Manifestation Magick: A Guide to Unlocking Abundance During the Solstice

Graboids and Garland: The Ultimate Tremors-Themed Christmas Guide

12 Nights of Holiday Magic

The Power of Pause: 60-Second Mindfulness Practices

The Quick Reset: How to Reclaim Your Life After Burnout

The Shadow Eater: A Tale of Despair and Survival

The Micro-Mastery Method: Transform Your Skills in Just Minutes a Day

Reclaiming Time: How to Live More by Doing Less

Chronovore: The Eternal Nexus

The Mind Reset: Unlocking Your Inner Peace in a Chaotic World

Confidence Code: Building Unshakable Self-Belief

Baby the Vampire Terrier
Baby the Vampire Terrier's Christmas Adventure
Celestial Streams: The Content Creator's Astrology Manual
The Wealth Whisperer: Unlocking Abundance with Everyday Actions
The Energy Equation: Maximize Your Output Without Burning Out
The Happiness Algorithm: Science-Backed Steps to Joyful Living
Stress-Free Success: Achieving Goals Without Anxiety
Mindful Wealth: The New Blueprint for Financial Freedom
The Festive Flavors of New Year: A Culinary Celebration
The Master's Gambit: Keys of Eternal Power
Shadowed Secrets: Groundhog Day Mysteries
Beneath the Burrow: Lessons from the Groundhog
Spring's Whispers: The Groundhog's Prediction
The Limitless Mindset: Unlock Your Untapped Potential
The Focus Funnel: How to Cut Through Chaos and Get Results
Bold Moves: Building Courage to Live on Your Terms
The Daily Shift: Simple Practices for Lasting Transformation
The Quarter-Life Reset: Thriving in Your 20s and 30s
The Art of Shadowplay: Building Your Own Personal Myth
The Eternal Loop: Finding Purpose in Repetition
Burrowing Wisdom: Life Lessons from the Groundhog
Shadow Work: A Groundhog Day Perspective
Love in Bloom: 5-Minute Romantic Gestures
The Shadowspell Codex: Secrets of Forbidden Magick
The Burnout Cure: Finding Balance in a Busy World
The Groundhog Prophecy: Unlocking Seasonal Secrets
Nog Tales: The Spirited History of Eggnog
Six More Weeks: Embracing Seasonal Transitions
The Lumivian Chronicles: Fragments of the Fifth Dimension
Money on Your Mind: A Beginner's Guide to Wealth
The Focus Fix: Breaking Through Distraction

January's Spirit Keepers: Mystical Protectors of the Cold
Creativity Unchained: Unlocking Your Wildest Ideas in 2025
Manifestation Mastery: 365 Days to Rewrite Your Reality
The Groundhog's Mirror: Reflecting on Change
The Weeping Angels' Christmas Curse
Burrowed in Time: A Groundhog Day Journey
Heartbeats: Poems to Share with Your Valentine
Dino Wicca: The Sacred Grimoire of Prehistoric Magick
Courage of the Pride: Finding Your Inner Roar
The Lion's Leap: Bold Moves for Big Results
Healthy Hustle: Achieving Without Overworking
Practical Manifesting: Turning Dreams into Reality in 2025
Jurassic Pharaohs: Unlocking the Magick of Ancient Egypt and Dino Wicca
The Happiness Equation: Small Changes for Big Joy
The Confidence Compass: Finding Your Inner Strength
Whispers in the Hollow: Tales of the Forgotten Beasts
Echoes from the Hollow: The Return of Forgotten Beasts
The Hollow Ascendant: The Rise of the Forgotten Beasts
The Relationship Reset: Building Better Connections
Mastering the Morning: How to Win the Day Before 8 AM
The Shadow's Dance: Groundhog Day Symbolism
Cupid's Kitchen: Quick Valentine's Day Recipes
Valentine's Day on a Budget: Love Without Breaking the Bank
Astrocraft: Aligning the Stars in the World of Minecraft
Forecasting Life: Groundhog Day Reflections
Bleeding Hearts: Twisted Tales of Valentine's Terror
Herbal Smoke Revolution: The Ultimate Guide to Nature's Cigarette Alternative
Winter's Wrath: The Complete Survival Blueprint for Extreme Freezes.
The Groundhog's Shadow: A Tale of Seasons
Burrowed Insights: Wisdom from the Groundhog

Sensual Strings: The Art of Erotic Bondage
Whispered Flames: Unlocking the Power of Fire Play
Forgotten Shadows: A Guide to Cryptids Lost to Time
Six Weeks of Secrets: Groundhog Day's Hidden Messages
Shadows and Cycles: Groundhog Day Reflections
The Art of Love Letters: Crafting the Perfect Message
Romantic Getaways at Home: Turning Your Space into Paradise
Purrfect Brews: A Cat Lover's Guide to Coffee and Companionship
The Groundhog's Wisdom: Timeless Lessons for Modern Life
The Shadow Oracle: Groundhog Day as a Predictor
Emerging from the Burrow: A Journey of Renewal
The Language of Love: Learning Your Partner's Love Style
Authorpreneur: The Ultimate Blueprint for Writing, Publishing, and Thriving as an Author
Weathering the Seasons: Groundhog Day Perspectives
Valentine's Day Magic: A Guide to Romantic Rituals
The Shadow Chronicles: Stories of Groundhog Day
Love and Laughter: Fun Games for Valentine's Day
AstroRealty: Unlocking the Stars for Property Success
The Groundhog's Path: A Guide to Seasonal Balance
Groundhog Day Diaries: Reflections in the Shadow
The Groundhog's Light: Illuminating the Path Ahead
Valentine's Traditions from Around the World
AI Wealth Revolution: Unlocking the Trillionaire Mindset
Love Rekindled: Reigniting Passion in Relationships
Single and Thriving: Self-Love on Valentine's Day
Emerald Legends: Mystical Tales of Ireland
Green Alchemy: Harnessing Nature's Magic
The Hearts of Horror: A Valentine's Day Nightmare
The Leprechaun's Guide to Wealth and Wisdom
Dancing with the Sidhe: Celebrating the Otherworld

Shamrocks and Shadows: Mysteries of the Green Isle

Emerald Energy: Harnessing Luck and Growth

The Gingerbread Golem's Valentine: A Sweetheart's Guide to Love and Enchantment

The Celtic Knot: Weaving Life and Destiny

Green Fire: Elemental Magic for St. Patrick's Day

Clover Chronicles: Finding Your Inner Luck

Ireland's Mystical Creatures: A Field Guide

Gingerbread Golem's Love Almanac

Prowl and Thrive: The Lion's Guide to Success

Love Alchemy: Transforming Your Life Through Heart Energy

WORLD DOMINATION: Woman's Rule 3:The New Life

The Midnight Rose: A Guide to Lunar Love Spells

The Forbidden Letters: Writing Your Own Love Prophecy

Luck and Lore: St. Patrick's Day for Modern Mystics

The Green Path: A Pagan Celebration of Renewal

The Dark Architect's Guide to Reprogramming Reality

Prankster's Paradise: A Guide to Harmless Hijinks

Manifest Your Reality: The Law of Attraction Simplified

The TARDIS Owner's Manual: Understanding the Doctor's Ship: *A complete guide to the TARDIS, its technology, secrets, and mysteries*

Starlit Romance: Astrology Secrets for Finding True Love

The Time Lord's Atlas: A Complete Guide to the Whoniverse: ***A breakdown of the locations, planets, and dimensions explored in Doctor Who***

Sweetheart Shadows: The Dark Side of Love and Attraction

February Fire: Reigniting Passion in Every Area of Life

The Self-Love Toolkit: 5 Ways to Embrace Who You Are

February Sparks: Ignite Your Dreams in 28 Days

March to Success: A 31-Day Action Blueprint

Ancient Paths: The 13 Sacred Principles of Dino Wicca

Echoes of Tomorrow: Navigating the AI Revolution
The Wellness Blueprint: Balancing Mind, Body, and Soul
Green Horizons: Sustainable Living for a Better Tomorrow
The AI Wealth Code: How to Make Millions with Automation
AI-Powered Creativity: Writing, Art, and Music for Profit
Extinction Rites: Rebirthing Your Soul Through Prehistoric Magick
Sacred Serpents tarot
Celestial Enchantment blank journal
Star Strains
Culinary Journeys: Exploring Global Flavors at Home
The Hollowvale Curse
The Hollowvale Harvest
The Egg of Transformation: Awakening Your Inner Power
Blooming Into Power: A Wiccan Guide to Spring Awakening
The Nightmare Nexus: The Third Doctor's Perilous Haunting
Digital Detox: Reclaiming Your Life in a Connected World
Ostara's Path: Walking the Spiral of Renewal
The Sacred Hare
Financial Freedom: Building Wealth in the Modern Age
Spring's Cauldron: Stirring the Waters of Change
The Hollowvale Pact
Quantum Consciousness: The Science of Reality Shifting
The Hollowvale Hunger
The Sacred Waters Within: A Witch's Guide to Hydrocephalus Magick
The Raven's Nest: Building a Life of Unshakable Stability
AI and the Human Mind: The Future of Intelligence
The Hollowvale Reckoning
Timeless Love: Building and Maintaining Lasting Relationships
The Raven's Roar: Unlocking Unstoppable Confidence
Raven Sight: Awakening Intuition and Inner Wisdom

The Butterfly Effect: Small Changes, Big Transformations

Taming the Boogeyman: How to Conquer Your Inner Fears

The Magick of Green: Awakening Earth's Energy in You

The Entrepreneurial Mindset: Secrets to Business Success

The Hollowvale End

The Shadow Luck Ritual: Reclaiming Power from Your Dark Side

Spring Magick for Beginners: A Simple Guide to Seasonal Energy Work

Doctor Who: The Hollowvale Conundrum

The March of Miracles: Unlocking Synchronicities in Spring

Unveiling the Cosmos: A Guide to Stargazing and Space Exploration

The Ultimate Guide to Surviving an Economic Collapse

The AI Gold Rush: How to Profit from the AI Revolution

Bastet's Shadow: The Hidden Power of Feline Magick

The Bastet Codex: Unlocking the Goddess's Magickal Secrets

Purring Spells: Harnessing Bastet's Healing Frequencies

Bastet's Nine Lives: Rebirth, Transformation, and Immortality Spells

Primal Currents: Hydrocephalus Magick in the Path of Dino Wicca

The Digital Gold Rush: Mastering E-Commerce and Online Sales

Future Shock: Adapting to the Next Decade of Change

The Quantum Mindset: Think Like a Billionaire

Sacred Motherhood: Awakening the Divine Feminine Within

The Mother's Spellbook: Enchantments for Love, Protection, and Prosperity

The Witch's Guide to Parenting: Raising Empowered and Intuitive Children

The Magick of Motherhood: Reclaiming Your Power Through Rituals

The Pagan Path to Self-Love: A Goddess's Guide to Worth and Confidence
Wild Woman Magick: Unleashing Your Primal Power
The Money Magnet Blueprint: Unlocking Unlimited Wealth
Biohacking 101: Unlock Your Body's Full Potential
The Wild Father: A Pagan Guide to Strength and Wisdom
The Sacred Masculine: Unlocking Your Inner Power
The Druid's Compass
The Warrior's Mindset
The Father's Fire
Odin's Path
Ancestral Bonds
The House That Whispers
The Magician's Code
The Wild Hunt
The Green Man's Path
The Altar of Success
The Shadow and the Sword
The High Priestess's Guide to Energy Healing
The Lunar Mother
The Sacred Self-Care Grimoire
The Womb Wisdom Codex
The Wheel of the Mother
The Witch's Guide to Manifestation
The Q2 Reset
The Ultimate Guide to AI-Powered Passive Income
Escape the 9-5
AI Feline Fortunes
The Tear-Stained Grimoire
Razorblade Runes
Cemetery Sirens
The Midnight Wristwatch
The Town That Forgets

AI Horror & Creepypasta
The Hollow Frequency
The Breach Echo
The Quiet Between Worlds
The Sigil of Tharan-Khul
Summon the Vault of Y'ha'ten
The Becoming Codex
The Profit of Az'ra-nar
The Drowned Logos
Echoes of the Eldritch Will
The Deep Ledger
Necronomicon of Networth
Covenant of the Wealthwyrm
The Whisperer's Manifesto
The Rites of Azh-K'luth
The Ark of the Crawling Coin
The Tithe of Shadows
Inkheart Abyss
The Timewinds of Y'ha-nthlei
The Spiral Labyrinth of Azag-Nirrh
The Gallifreyan Heresy of the Black Pharaoh
The Psalms of Nyog-Sotha
Black Rain Alchemy
The Infinite Maw
The Entropic Blueprint
The Oracle of Sh'guul
The Book of Breach
The Drowned Saint's Testament
Dreamcraft of the Sleeper God
The Silence Market
Cthonomics: The Dark Wealth Algorithm
Invocation of the Ten-Eyed King
Wealthbound to the Wyrm Below

Become the Unnameable
Codex of the Sovereign Flame
Rituals of Relentless Becoming
The Shadow Ascends
The Eyes Beneath You
The Will That Wakes Worlds
Silence Is a Weapon
The Mirror That Screams
The Whisper Between Moments
The Mind That Devours Fear
The Myth of the Finished Self
The Architect of Your Madness
The Voice You've Buried
The Discipline of Madness
Stormborn: Awakening Your Inner Tempest
The Mind That Ate Time
Unbind Your Becoming
The Pact You Owe Yourself
The Devourer's Diet
The Acid That Carves the Path
The Tower You Must Burn
The Breath Between Worlds
Speak Like the Deep
The Labyrinth Within
The Spine of the Sea God
Rejection Is a Portal
The Crown You Refused
The Scar Is the Spell
The Lightless Flame
The Habit of Becoming Horrific
ChickenJockey Chaos
The Gatekeeper Within
You Are Not Your Name

The Compass of the Mad
The Archive of Unsent Letters
What the Mirror Can't Show You
The Knife You Needed
Worship Nothing, Become Everything
The Other Voice
The Body the World Forgot
The Vein of the Void
The Black Bone Codex
The Puzzle of the Hidden Self (Millennium Puzzle)
The Eye That Sees the Lie *(Millennium Eye)*
The Ring of Return (Millennium Ring)
The Rod of Relentless Will *(Millennium Rod)*
The Tally of the Soul (Millennium Tauk/Necklace)
The Key to the Locked Timeline (Millennium Key)
The Scale of Sacred Decisions (Millennium Scales)
Inferno Bites: The UnOfficial Minecraft Lava Cookbook
Rot in the Attic
Prana: The Hidden Force of Your Infinite Self
The Shadow Realm Within: Transforming Darkness Into Destiny
The Borderland Collapse
Claws of Protection: Bastet's Defensive Magick
Mr. Ring-a-Ding's Madness
Yugioh Astrology: Celestial Deckcraft and Duel Destiny (2026–2027 Edition)
The Seal You Signed: Unlocking the Power You Once Feared
The Puzzle of Infinite Minds: Unlocking the Mentalism Hidden Within
The Eye That Mirrors the All: Secrets of Inner Reflection
Doctor Who: The Toymaker's Broadcast
The Rod of Eternal Flow: Commanding the Currents of Vibration

Golden Eyes of Bastet: Enhancing Psychic Vision
The Key of Dual Forces: Balance Within the Polarity
The Scales of Living Rhythm: Timing the Dance of Life
The Necklace of Hidden Cause: Weaving the Webs of Fate
The Ring of Secret Masters: Rising Through the All Within All
Daggers of the Dying Deep
Bastet's Wealth and Fortune Magick: Prosperity Rituals of the Goddess
The Tide that Speaks
The Scrolls of Petosiris: 13 Rituals from the Feathered Eye
Petosiris and the Living Plague of Osirion
Feline Fire: Bastet's Passion and Love Magick
The Star Altar of Petosiris
Bastet's Whiskers: Supernatural Sensory Magick
The Bastet Grimoire
Feeding the Shadows
The Mouthless Prayer
The Spiral Wound
Becoming the Ibis: Lessons from Petosiris's Mind
The Crimson Coven: Cola Magick for Sweet Dominion
Sacred Cat's Paw
The Soda Zodiac: A Flavor for Every Sign
Covenant of the Crawling Flame
The Ink of Ish'Zur
Frothroot: The Thirst That Ate the World
The Golden Glyphs of Prosperity
The Etherbind Codex
Echoes of the Resistance: Reclaiming the You That Survived
Harnessed Minds: Breaking Free from Mental Control
The Eyes in the Smoke
Rootwake: The Carbon Covenant
Skitter Logic: Unlearning the Fear That Built You

Doctor Who: The World That Froths
Rootwake: The Fizz That Rewrites Flesh
Rootwake: Frothfather of the World
The Holly Pact: Blood Beneath the Mistletoe
The 2nd Mass Principle: Building Unbreakable Tribes
Web of Wits: A Survival Guide to Encounters with Anasi the Spider (Aunt Nancy)
The Hexbreaking Handbook: Effective Spells to Remove Curses
Pop Alchemy: Transform Your Life One Sip at a Time
The Mason Code: Leading in Unleadable Times
Petosiris and the Fifth Chamber of Thoth
The Ether Seed Within
The Parent of Tomorrow
Petosiris's Pyramid of Perpetual Wealth
Unlearn the World
Grimoire of the Hollow Tongue
Zodiac Weeds: Finding Your Strain Through the Stars
Aquarius Rises in the Bank
The Sugar God's Smile
The Skinclock Reversal: Biohacking the Face of Time
Debtburn: How to Obliterate What You Owe Forever
The Ice Cream Oracle: What Your Cone Says About Your Future
Silence Is Sovereignty: The Power of Being Unreadable
The Wind That Whispers Through Stone
Path of the Four Directions
Doctor Who: The Maestro's Symphony of Endings
Oxygen Grail: Breathing to Undo the Clock
Zodiacal Collapse: When Stars Devour Time
Teachings from the Red Sand Silence
Doctor Who: Omega – The Broken Equation
Memory Wipe Your Past: Start Over Like a MiB

Mitochondria Prime: Ignite the Core of Youth

A Nest of Roaches

Grub from the Galaxy: MiB Recipes You'll Never Forget

Whiskers of Power: Bastet's Guide to Inner Sovereignty

The Gift Must Cost Them: Negotiation Through Unequal Exchange

The Worm Guys' Wealth Code: Hustle Like an Alien

Bug Out: The Edgar Method for Ruthless Goal Setting

Weaving Life with Spiderwoman's Pattern

Doctor Who: The Rani's Renaissance

How to Get a Job (If You're a Puppygirl)

Speak Through Others: The Art of Proxy Power

T-Rex Your Trauma: Reclaim the Power of Your Primal Self

The Black Briefcase: How MiB Stay Wealthy in Silence

The Thirst Beyond Reason: Understanding Diabetes Insipidus From the Inside Out

Backwoods Witchcraft for Billionaires: The Pagan Path from Dirt Roads to Gold Roads

The Moonshine Grimoire: Fermented Spells for Abundance

The Nameless Geometry

The Wraith's Mixtape: Spellcasting with Songs of Sorrow

The Gallifreyan Gentleman: Silent Wealth, Sonic Confidence, and the Doctor's Code of Living

Sugar Water Confidence

Dino Totems: Spirit Guides from Earth's First Gods

Pumpkin Sigils & Ritual Smoke

The Hózhó Compass

The Distortus Discipline – Order from Inner Mutation

Witchcraft for the Cold-Blooded Soul

Moonlight Over the Blessingway

Water, Interrupted: When the Body Forgets How to Hold On

Deformed but Divine: Embracing Your Asymmetry

Hexes in the Henhouse: The Farm Witch's Guide to Power

The Reversed Flame: A Grimoire of Inverted Power

Salt, Cells, and Sanity: Reclaiming Balance with Diabetes Insipidus

King of the Broken: Crowning the Flawed Self

Moonlight Scars: Emo Moon Magick and the Art of Lunar Sorrow

Noose Spells: Magick of the Hanging Rope

The Goth Cathedral: Rituals of the Broken and Beautiful

The Cretaceous Codex: Dino Spirits and Fossil Magick

The Turkey Bones Ritual

Nine Lives of Manifestation: Unlocking Bastet's Reality Codes

Chaos Muscles: Building Strength from Twisted Pain

Emo Blood Magick: The Veins of Power

The 3AM Flood: Nighttime Urination, Sleep Loss, and the DI Spiral

The Silence Between the Stars

The Lemon Method: Sour Your Way to Success

Starlit Sovereign

The Rite of Twelve Gates: Walking the Gates of the Duat.

Cornbread and Conjure: Recipes for Riches and Rootwork

The Black Rose Rituals: Emo Love Spells and Obsession Magick

The Eternal Goodbye: Death Magick and Rebirth Rituals

Sinkrot: The Drain That Remembers

The Hybrid Mindset: Thinking Beyond Evolution

Bone Dry: Navigating Dehydration Before It Breaks You

Wreathcraft: Winter Sigils and Yuletide Spells

The Rite of Twelve Mouths

S'mores of the Damned: Haunted Recipes for Halloween Night

Rethink the Drink: A Beverage Survival Guide for DI Warriors

The Shadow Chord: Guitar Magick and Sonic

Malformed Yet Majestic: Leading When You Feel Wrong Inside

The Cursed Diary: Ink-Stained Spells of the Emo Soul

Anxiety Off Switch: Emergency Reset for a Fried Nervous System

The Energy Heist: How to Take Back Your Life from Drainers

Beyond the Bathroom: Rebuilding Your Social Life With DI

Coyote's Gift for Decision Makers

Ghoul-Goo: Spooky S'mores You'll Die For

Echoes in the Mirror: Scrying and Self-Destruction Magick

Thread and Thorn: Stitching Spells from Rural Cloth

The Mogwai Mind: Building Untouchable Wealth from Small Ideas

Be Your Own Guide: Trust Your Inner Compass

Hormones in Chaos: The Endocrine Puzzle of Diabetes Insipidus

ChronoCleanse: Detox Your Biological Timeline

The Limb You Hide Is the One That Saves You

Leaves, Bones, and Whisper Spells

The Dinosaur Mindset: Prehistoric Tactics for Modern Wealth

Clawing Back Control: A Bastet Method for Boundaries and Empowerment

Samhain Codes of the Forgotten

Orange Alchemy: The Autumnal Spellbook

Monster Within, Master Without

The Sigil That Sleeps

Hearthcraft: Yule Hearth Sigils and Winter Warmth Spells

Temple of the Purring Moon: Rituals from Bastet's Lineage

When the Earth Remembers Your Footsteps

Food for Mood: Eat to Heal Depression, Not Just Survive It

Witch of the Kudzu Vine: Southern Pagan Wealth Secrets

The Invisible Diagnosis: Advocating for Yourself With DI

The Coffin's Lullaby: Sleep Magick and Nightmares as Portals
Ashes of the Will: Rituals for Erasing the Self
The Fracture Rite: Shattering the Magickal Core
Funeral Candles: The Art of Emo Flame Magick
The Black Grimoire: A Blank Ritual for Writing in Absence
Phantom Thirst: A Halloween Survival Guide for Diabetes Insipidus
The Hollow Crown: Emo Royalty and Magick of the Outcast King
Sandpainting for the Soul
Falling Into Balance: Using the Extra Hour to Recalibrate Life
100 Southern Superstitions That Still Work
The DI Child: A Parent's Guide to Raising Hydrated, Happy Kids
The Jungle of Shame: Escaping the Hidden Lab of Doubt
The Witch's Toast: S'mores Spells and Creepy Confections
The Hoodoo Pantry: Spells from the Mason Jar
The Immortal Fortune: Secret Wealth Lessons from Captain Jack Harkness
The Specter's Embrace: Magick for Channeling Ghostly Lovers
Grateful Waters: A Thanksgiving Survival Guide for Diabetes Insipidus
The Seizure Gospel
Harvestbind: Autumn Sigils and Samhain Spells
Doctor Who: The Algorithmic Awakening
Silent Nights, Steady Waters: A Christmas Survival Guide for Diabetes Insipidus
The Extra Hour Effect: How One Hour Can Transform Everything
Blade Between the Breaths
Running with the Mountain Shadows
Echoes of the Failed Experiment – Becoming a Living Legacy

Swamp Witches & River Ghosts: Real Southern Hauntings

Cornbread Prophecies: Magical Recipes from a Southern Table

Doctor Who: The Signal in the Star

Bloomcraft: Spring Sigils and Equinox Enchantments

Vanisher: How to Disappear from the Internet Without Losing Your Life

The Ultimate Christmas Cookie Cookbook

The Unbreakable Parent: How to Mentally Survive Raising Kids in a Broken World

Time Debt: How to Reclaim the Hours You Didn't Know You Lost

One Month, One Million: Unconventional Cash Creation Tactics

Doctor Who: The Cyber Conversion Protocol

Black Friday Frenzy: The Art of Finding Hidden Online Deals

The Grimoire Buried Under the Apple Tree

Digital Couponing Masterclass: Your Step-by-Step Guide to Black Friday Savings

The Fire Inside the Flint

Shadows on the Ceiling: The Emo Guide to Astral Magick

The Bone-Eaters Beneath Us

Black Friday Bundle Blueprint: Creating Irresistible Product Packages for Maximum Sales

Thirteen Nights of Unbinding

Doctor Who: Engines of Influence

Pumpkin Spice Alchemy: Recipes of Fire and Frost

When Raptor Met Rexy: Prehistoric Lessons in Wild Romance

Oblivion's Candle: Burn the Path Behind You

Campfire Curses and Chocolate: A Halloween S'mores Grimoire

The Wallet That Wasn't Mine: Breaking Free from Inherited Scarcity
The Cola Zodiac: What Your Fizz Says About Your Fate
Frostfire Fortune: Unlocking Winter's Hidden Prosperity
Signal Jamming: Detox Your Brain from Info Overload
The Dust of the Forgotten Rite
The Golden Cat Sigils: Drawing Power in Bastet's Name
Mud Magick: The Prosperity of Getting Dirty
Savory Spicefall: Beyond the Pumpkin Pie
Pumpkin Spice Apothecary Kitchen
The Pumpkin Spice Economy: Turning Trends into Billions
The Ember Veil: 13 Nights of Fire Magick
Financial Freeze: When Earning Triggers Panic
The Gingerbread Alchemist: Sweet Recipes with a Twist
Biosynth Power: Programming Yourself from Scratch
Echoes from the Talking Circle
Truffle Alchemy: Fungus of Fortune
Spores of Power: The Truffle Witch's Handbook
Doctor Who: The Tower That Speaks
The Mycelium Veil: Truffle Magick Unbound
Broke But Ashamed: Healing the Shame Wound of Debt
The Evergreen Mind: Growth Through Winter Stillness
The Black Veil Truffle Rite
The Voice Beneath Symbols
Witchlight on the Bayou: Swamp Spells for Sovereignty
I Grew Up Poor and Now I Sabotage My Success
The Lantern of Hollow Souls
Shutdown Survival: A Citizen's Guide to Thriving When Government Stops
When Abundance Feels Like a Threat: Healing the Hidden Fears of Enough
The Scarecrow Grimoire
Owls of the October Veil

Candlewax and Curses: A Halloween Spellbook
Excavating the Inner Fossil – Transforming Fossilized Thoughtforms into Tools of Power
The Yule Witch's Spellbook: Magick for the Holiday Season
Haunted Christmas: Ghost Stories for Winter Nights
The Christmas Survival Guide: Thriving Through the Chaos
The Bone Orchard Rites
Haunted Commerce: The Ghost in the Marketplace
When Money Triggers the Inner Child
Silent Night with the Silence: A Christmas Thriller
The Lightning Crown: Living and Leading Through Seizures
TARDIS Tidings: Festive Stories from the Whoniverse
Autumn Reset: Slowing Down Without Falling Behind
The Trillion Dollar Soul: Rewriting the Currency of Reality
Truffle Eclipse Magick
Micro-Manifestations: Quick Magick That Works
5-Minute Rituals for Busy Witches
The Marshmallow Massacre: Halloween Treats with a Sinister Twist
Blood and Blackberry Thorns
Magickal Mornings: Rituals for a Blessed Christmas Day
Embers of the All-Hallows Fire
The Pumpkin Market Collapse
The Hour You Gained: Transforming Time Into Power
The Chamber Must Be Sealed: Mastering the Power of Controlled Access
The Cursed Manuscript of Petosiris
The Festive Hearth: Creating Holiday Traditions
Darkness Rising: Thriving as Nights Grow Longer
Harvesting Time: Turning the Year's End Into Your New Beginning
Petosiris and the 13th Zodiac Key
Wagewound: When Paychecks Become Identity Prisons

Walls That Watch
The Silent Feast: Rituals of Power in the Longest Night
The Distortus Legacy : Becoming a Deformed King in a Perfect World
The Hollow Masks
The Gratitude Furnace: Forging Gold from Thanks
Feast of Inner Gold: Eating for Energy and Enlightenment
Haunted Commerce: The Season of Spending Spirits
Fear Bonds: How Panic Creates Profit
Black Friday E-Commerce Playbook: Sales Tactics to Skyrocket Your Holiday Revenue
Budgeting for Black Friday: A Holiday Savings Planner
Haunting the Harvest Moon
The Warrior's Water: Emergency Preparedness for People With DI
The First Sip of the Year: A New Year's Survival Guide for Diabetes Insipidus
Doctor Who: The Thirteenth Node
The Unseen Struggle: Mental Health, Anxiety, and Chronic Thirst
The Hearth's Hidden Ledger: Counting Energies as Currency
The Gift Alchemist: Turning Any Offering Into Gold
The Papyrus of the Bound Spirit
The Magick of Leftovers: Transmutation in the Fridge
Frost and Fortune: Christmas Wealthcraft for the Modern Magus
Last-Minute Gifts: Creative Ideas on a Budget
10 Secrets to Surviving Holiday Crowds
The Witch's Dow Jones
The Witches' Graveyard Shift
Pumpkin Sigils: Carving Rites for Midnight Power
The Secret Shopper's Black Friday Guide: How to Get Early Access and VIP Deals

Fever in the Foundation

The Neuralyzer Reset: Reprogram Your Morning Routine

Lightning Lessons of the White Painted Woman

The Enchanted Snowflake

The Magic Sip: Surviving Disney Parks with Diabetes Insipidus

The One Who Draws Through You

Santa's Secrets: A Magical Holiday Planner

Silent Bells, Loud Miracles: Self-Help for the Season of Stillness

The Sugar Spell Codex: Confectionary Magick of Christmas

Autumn Hexcraft: Fallen Leaves, Fallen Barriers

Sleep Like a Fortress: Build a Life Where Insomnia Can't Survive

Nowhere Was Ever Home

Christmas Under the Stars: A Celestial Holiday Guide

Rentproof: How to Never Be Evicted Again

Workless: Escape the 9-5 Without Being Broke

The Gilded Gift: A Wealth Altar for Christmas Morning

The Black Friday Grimoire

The Hollowing: Ceremonies of Spiritual Collapse

Doctor Who: The Nameless Signal

Where the Eagle Hides His Courage

The Dwarf Tyrant's Ascent: Claiming Power in a World of Giants

The Currency of the Dead: Trading with Spectral Bankers

The Icebound Witch: Survival and Magick in the Cold

The Emergency Money Mind: Constant Crisis, Zero Calm

Thirst & Roses: A Valentine's Survival Guide for Diabetes Insipidus

Springing Into Clarity: Mastering the Energy Shift of Daylight Saving

Speed of the Nanotyrant: Agile Strategies for Life's Hunt

The 90-Day Reset: A Science-Backed Guide to Reinvent Yourself Before the New Year

The Coil of Thorns

Timegates Unleashed

Dopamine Fasting 2.0: Rewiring Your Brain in a World of Overstimulation

The Nanotyrannus Mutation: Embracing Your Differentiated Form

Unwritten January: How to Use the Blank Page of the Year to Re-Author Your Life

Feast of the Forgotten Spirits: Ancestor Magick for the Holidays

The Burnout Codex: A System for Thriving Beyond Stress

I Don't Deserve to Have Money

When the King Doesn't See You: The Shadow Predator's Guide

The Reset Ritual :A Guide to Shedding Last Year's Weight—Emotional and Physical—by Spring Cleaning Your Soul

Calendar Alchemy: Learn to Bend Time and Productivity around Your Natural Rhythms

The Mirror Contract: A One-Sentence Agreement with Yourself that Unlocks Real Change

The Nile Formula: Sacred Flow for Millionaire Minds

Forward Momentum: Productivity Rituals for the Lost Hour

Harvest Gold: Wealth Magick of Pumpkin Spice Commerce

The Magick of Christmas Lights: Illuminating Holiday Rituals

Cranberry Crown: Royal Self-Worth through Ritual Meals

Petosiris and the Worms of the Feathered Throne

The Evergreen Equation: Self-Help for Sustained Growth

The Rain Will Wash Us Away: Emo Weather Magick

Snowlight Shadows: Magick Under Frozen Stars

Doctor Who: Merger of Empires

The Light Within the Feast: Magickal Wealth of Yuletide Flame

Momentum Machines: Small Habits Designed to Snowball into Unstoppable Forward Motion

Calm Spells: Magickal Solutions for Anxiety Relief

Santa's Final List: The Naughty Never Leave

The Mystic's Guide to Banishing Worry

The Silence Dividend: Turning Quiet Mornings into Compounding Growth All Year

Charmed Stillness: Rituals to Ease the Mind

Blood Spiral Ascension

The Vanishing Heart Invocation

Crystal Calm: Harnessing Stones for Anxiety

The Nano Tyrant Code: Strength in the Small Predator

The Energy Ledger: Accounting Methods for Vitality, Not Just Money

Snowglobe Mindset: Shake Up Your Thoughts, Settle Into Peace

The Weight of the Feather: Anubis's Codes for Soul Balance

Pocket Peppermint Power: Tiny Rituals for Big Holiday Energy

Shadowkeeper of the Golden Jackal: Anubis's Path to Energetic Protection

The Witch's Breath: Anxiety Relief Through Magickal Breathing

Get Some Tarot cards: https://www.makeplayingcards.com/sell/apophis-occult-shop

Get some shirts: https://www.bonfire.com/store/apophis-shirt-emporium/

<u>Instagrams:</u>
@apophis_enterprises,
@apophisbookemporium,
@apophisscardshop
Twitter: @apophisenterpr1
Tiktok:@apophisenterprise
Youtube: @sg1fan23477
Hive: @sg1fan23477
CheeLee: @SG1fan23477

Podcast: Apophis Chat Zone: https://open.spotify.com/show/5zXbrCLEV2xzCp8ybrfHsk?si=fb4d4fdbdce44dec

Newsletter: https://apophiss-newsletter-27c897.beehiiv.com/

If you want to support me or see posts of other projects that I have come over to: **buymeacoffee.com/mpetchinskg**

I post there daily several times a day

Get your Dinowicca or Christmas themed digital products, especially Santa Raptor songs and other musics. Here: **https://sg1fan23477.gumroad.com**

Apophis Yuletide Digital has not only digital Christmas items, but it will have all things with Dinowicca as well as other Digital products.

www.ingramcontent.com/pod-product-compliance
Lightning Source LLC
LaVergne TN
LVHW022015200926
848481LV00007B/2395
* 9 7 9 8 3 3 0 5 8 4 6 1 1 *